Contents

4...snip and stick

6...secret scrapbook

8...pretty pots

10...party decorations

12...paper beads

14...paper pulp

16...hide and seek!

18...fruity cakes!

20...clown hats

22...wrap it up!

24...tips and tricks

snip and stick

Did you know you can make a picture using just paper, without paints or pencils? Plan it out in your head first. Will your picture have people, animals, flowers or buildings, or will it be a pattern?

1 Collect together lots of different kinds of paper – brown paper, newspaper, tissue, coloured paper and paper from magazines.

2 Use a large sheet of paper for the background. When you have decided what your picture is going to be, you can start cutting or tearing paper shapes. Always use safety scissors like the ones in the picture.

let's play with
Paper

Ivan Bulloch & Diane James

Created by
Two-Can Publishing Ltd
346 Old Street
London EC1V 9NQ

Art Director Ivan Bulloch
Editor Diane James
Illustrator Emily Hare
Photographer Daniel Pangbourne
Models Imaarl, Alicia, Kaz, Maryam, Cory, Jasmin, Abigail,
Kerri, Courtney, Eleanor, Shaniqua

First published by Two-Can Publishing Ltd in 1997
in association with Franklin Watts

Hardback ISBN 1-85434-515-X
Paperback ISBN 1-85434-517-6

Dewey Decimal Classification 745.54

Paperback 2 4 6 8 10 9 7 5 3 1

A catalogue record for this book is available from the British Library

Printed in Spain by Graficromo S.A

3 Lay your paper shapes in the right places to make your picture. Don't worry about changing your mind. Sometimes second or third ideas are best!

cut it out ...

4 When you are happy with how your paper picture looks, glue the shapes in place. Press all the shapes down firmly to stop the edges from curling up. You can use a rolling pin to help!

...and stick it down!

secret scrapbook

show me yours!

Where do you keep all your favourite pictures and photos? If the answer is in an untidy pile, or hidden away in a cardboard box, it's time you made yourself a scrapbook! Then you can stick your pictures in it and enjoy them whenever you feel like it.

1 Decide how many pages you want in your scrapbook. Cut the pages out of coloured paper, making sure they are all the same size.

2 Use a hole punch to make two holes on the side of each page. Make sure the holes are in the same place on every page. You can punch holes in two or three sheets at the same time.

OK! let's share secrets

3 Decorate the cover by sticking on shapes cut from coloured paper. Or you can use pictures cut from a magazine. Don't forget to ask first!

4 Cut two lengths of thin ribbon or cord. Stack your pages on top of each other with the cover on top. Thread the ribbons through the holes and tie a bow. Now you can start sticking things on the pages!

pretty pots

Here is an easy way to make an extra special gift! First you'll need a plant in a pot. Make sure the outside of the pot is clean and dry. Follow the instructions and make a colourful wrapper for the pot.

1 Measure round the top of your pot using a piece of string. Cut a strip of paper, about half as long again. The paper should be deep enough to cover the pot but let the flowers show.

2 Decorate the paper by gluing on simple shapes cut from different coloured paper. Press them down.

I made this just for you!

3 Start at one end of the strip and fold the paper backwards and forwards until you reach the other end. Make the folds exactly the same size each time.

4 Gently wrap the folded paper around the flower pot and glue the edges together. Your present is ready!

9

party decorations

All you have to do is make a few simple folds, a couple of snips with your scissors, and 'hey presto', you'll have some great decorations to cheer up the party!

don't pull too hard!

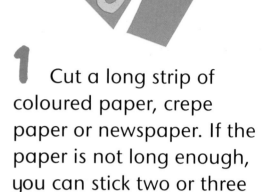

1 Cut a long strip of coloured paper, crepe paper or newspaper. If the paper is not long enough, you can stick two or three lengths together.

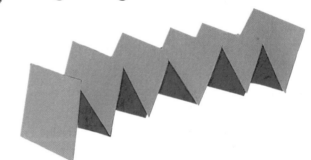

2 Start at one end of the strip, and fold the paper backwards and forwards until you reach the other end. The folded paper should be big enough to draw on half of a shape, for example, half a rabbit or half a butterfly shape.

3 Keep your paper folded up and draw half a shape on the top fold. The centre of the shape should go on the folded edge. Make sure that one part of the shape goes as far as the other edge.

just a bit higher!

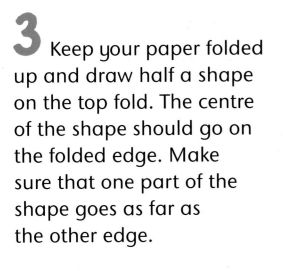

4 Ask a grown-up to help cut along your drawn lines, through all the layers. They must take care not to cut along the folded edge. Unfold your shape to make a long decoration!

11

paper beads

You won't need to spend all your pocket money on real jewellery when you find out how easy it is to make necklaces from bits of coloured paper! When you're not wearing your beads, hang them up to decorate your room.

1 Glue two different coloured sheets of paper together. Press them together firmly.

2 When the glue is dry, tear out long, thin triangles. Don't worry about the rough edges. Make as many triangles as you can from your sheet.

3 Start with the wide end of the triangle and wind it round and round a thick pencil. Be careful of the pencil lead. Stick the tip of the triangle down with a dab of glue. Slip the bead off the pencil. Make lots of beads in the same way.

4 Thread your beads on to thick cord or ribbon. Ask a friend to tie your necklace together at the back.

13

paper pulp

It's hard to believe, but you really can make a big bowl using just newspaper, water and some PVA glue. There are also lots of other things you can make when you know how to mix up this gooey paper pulp.

1 Tear four or five large sheets of newspaper into small pieces. Put them in a bucket and pour in enough water to cover them.

2 Leave the newspaper to soak overnight. Squish the pieces together with your hands and pour away the leftover water. Add three or four big squirts of PVA glue and mix well with a wooden spoon.

...for pencils!

perfect...

3 Use a large bowl as a mould. Cover it with clingfilm to stop the pulp sticking when it is dry. Take small handfuls of pulp and press them on to the mould.

4 When the mould is covered, leave the pulp to dry. This can take three or four days! Lift the paper bowl off the mould. Now you can paint your bowl in your favourite colours.

looking good!

15

hide and seek!

Would you like to be a black and white panda, or a spotty monster? You can be anything you like with the help of one of our jolly masks!

bet you can't guess who I am!

1 Cut out a mask shape, slightly wider than your face, from coloured card. Leave room for your nose to poke out at the bottom!

2 Ask a grown-up to measure how far apart your eyes are. Then they can cut holes in your mask so you can see out. Now it's time to decorate your mask.

3 Cut out shapes from coloured paper and glue them in place.

here comes the spotty monster!

4 Ask a grown-up to make a small hole either side of your mask. Poke a length of thin cord or ribbon through each hole and make a knot. Find a friend to help tie the mask around your head.

fruity cakes!

Paper cakes are a lot easier to make than the real thing. The only problem is you can't eat them! Think of all your favourite toppings – cream, chocolate, cherries, and add them to your cakes. Now give your dolls and teddies a special treat!

1 Make a collection of used cake-shaped boxes, round ones, square, rectangles, even triangles!

2 Draw round one of the boxes on a sheet of coloured paper. Cut out the shape and glue it on to the top of the box.

not for eating - just for fun!

3 Cut a long strip of coloured paper the same height as your box. Make small folds backwards and forwards along the strip. Put the strip around the box and tape the ends.

4 Have fun decorating the top of your cake! Think of food shapes. Cut them from coloured paper and glue them down.

clown hats

Why don't you turn yourself into a clown with a funny paper hat and curly paper hair! Add some colourful face paints and put on a funny act for your friends.

sad face clown!

1 Draw a large circle, about 45 cm in diameter, on a piece of coloured paper. Cut it out and fold it in half. Now cut down the folded line. Decorate one half by gluing on coloured paper shapes. Save the other half to make another hat later!

20

2 Gently curve your half circle into a cone shape. Tape the edges together. Ask a grown-up to make a hole either side of your hat. Thread a length of ribbon through each hole. Tie a knot to stop the ribbon sliding through.

3 Tape shredded paper round the inside of the hat, leaving a space at the front. Or, use thick wool.

happy face clown!

wrap it up!

Even the smallest present will look extra special if it's wrapped in paper you have designed yourself. Put the present in a cardboard box, as this will make it easier to wrap up. No one will guess what's inside!

1 Find a large sheet of plain wrapping paper, or coloured paper. It should be big enough to wrap round your box and overlap at either end.

2 Decide on a pattern and cut some shapes from a different coloured paper.

which one would you like?

3 Cut more paper shapes using different colours. Glue all the shapes on to the wrapping paper.

4 Put your present – in its box – in the middle of the sheet of paper. Wrap the long sides over and tape them in place. Tuck both ends in neatly and tape them down.

tips and tricks

Here are some of our favourite tips to help you with your paper craft.

1 Keep your collection of papers in a big envelope. Even scraps may be useful.

2 To make good, sharp folds, run your fingers up and down each fold carefully.

3 If something goes wrong, don't throw the paper away! Smooth it out and use it again!

4 Use scissors to cut a smooth edge to your paper shapes. If you want a rough edge, try tearing the paper carefully.

5 When you are gluing shapes on to a piece of paper, press them down firmly and wait until the glue is dry.

6 If you need extra strong paper, glue two layers of paper together to make a thicker sheet.